Katie Clemons

LET'S CELEBRATE YOUR STORY

My First
READING
JOURNAL

to:

from:

because:

TO LINDEN, MY INQUISITIVE FACT
FINDER. PROMISE YOU'LL ALWAYS
WONDER, "WHY?"

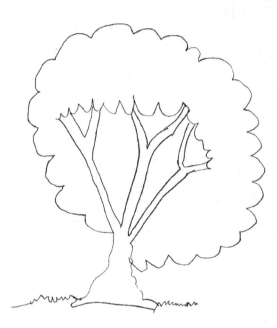 

Art by Niklas (age 7) and Linden (age 3)

FLYING Y

Flying Y LLC
PO Box 812
Livingston, MT 59047

Design and text by Katie Clemons.
Copyright ©2021 Flying Y LLC.
Published in the United States of America by Flying Y LLC.

https://katieclemons.com
Printed in USA

ISBN: 978-1-63336-047-1

BOOKS ARE JOY AWAITING US

Howdy Caring Adult,

Last night as my head sunk into my pillow, all I could recall was picnicking with my boys Niklas and Linden. They nibbled our summer smorgasbord in the shade while I read aloud Beverly Cleary's wonderful *Henry Huggins*. Henry had just received an exhilarating ride home in a police car when my boys leapt up and zoomed around the yard with loud squeals:

"Wheeee-oooooh! Whee-oooh!"

I love how books always have an enchanting way of connecting children with the world. Page by page, they discover people, ideas, places, and times they might not have experienced or understood. They learn more about themselves. They come upon more of the universe's magic and develop greater empathy.

I'm glad Henry is a dear friend at our house now. No matter how exhausted I become, I find that I never regret the time spent reading with my kids or observing how books spark their lives. Like countless parents, grandparents, and teachers, I've discovered that one of the best ways to further enrich a child's reading experience is to invite them to create a reading log.

An impactful reading log isn't just a checklist of books read. It's a memory book of seemingly ordinary characters' captivating adventures and a menagerie of discoveries. Writing also helps a child reflect on books they complete. They get to practice expressing themselves, while improving their penmanship and solidifying their memories of beautiful books.

Let this journal be your child's guidepost for exploring books they finish. You and your child can decide what types of books to log. Seven year-old Niklas records novels I read aloud. Your child might want to reflect on books they read aloud to you, beloved picture books, audiobooks, library books, or whatever sparks their imagination.

Progress is more important than perfection. We don't want to hinder a child's love of books with unobtainable timelines or emphases on flawless spelling and penmanship. **In this journal, let thoughtful creativity prevail.** Guide your child to work through the four sections of this journal however they suit your child:

★ **1. Fun guided prompts** invite your child to explore their reading life and rediscover their bookshelves or library. Pages 5 to 39.

★ **2. Color and cut activities** grant them a creativity opportunity to make fun bookish projects. Pages 40 to 47.

★ **3. A hand-drawn progress chart for 25 completed books** helps them witness their reading log progress at a glance. Each time a book is logged, they color in a cloud. Pages 48 and 49.

★ **4. A log for 25 books** enables them to record stories they've read and their responses. Pages 50 to 100.

Thanks for letting this journal and me join your journey. Write to me any time **howdy@katieclemons.com** (I answer all my mail), or tag me on social media **@katierclemons #katieclemonsjournals #myfirstjournals**.

Inside a book is always a wonderful world. Now let's celebrate your story!

Katie

P.S. Add to your child's reading life with the FREE exclusive printables and journaling activities my family enjoys:

https://katieclemons.com/a/2C8Z/

INSIDE

A BOOK IS A WONDERFUL WORLD

 HELLO STORY

This reading log belongs to

_____

- -

_____

I tell people to call me   Age

_____   _____

- - - - - - - - - - - - - - - - -   - - - - -

_____   _____

My address is

_____

- -

_____

- -

_____

Today I begin journaling!

_____

- -

_____

Here's a drawing or photograph of
ME READING
IN A COZY SPOT!

HERE'S WHERE
I LIKE TO READ

Color in favorites

At the library

Outside

In the bathroom

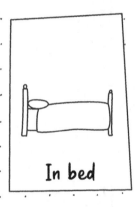

In bed

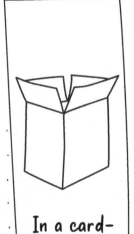

In a card-board box

On the couch

At _____'s home

In a bookshop

In the car

At school

At a desk or table

I LiKE TO READ ABOUT

1. _____

2. _____

3. _____

MY FAVORITE TiMES
TO READ ARE

In the morning	In the afternoon
At bedtime	A different time

THIS BOOK IS **AMAZING!**

Draw the
cover
and title

I've probably read it _____ times.

The book makes me feel

The author's name is

_____

- - - - - - - - - - - - - -

_____

It's a great book for kids who

_____

- - - - - - - - - - - - - -

_____

- - - - - - - - - - - - - -

I love this part of the book.

I GIVE IT ☆☆☆☆☆ STARS!

I REALLY LIKE THIS CHARACTER

If we could get together, we would

This character makes me think about

_____

- - - - - - - - - - - - - - - - - -

_____

_____

- - - - - - - - - - - - - - - - - -

_____

They're in this book

_____

- - - - - - - - - - - - - - - - - -

_____

Two ways our lives are similar

Two ways our lives are different

I think their adventures are 👍 / 👎 !

A FILL-IN-THE-BLANKS
SILLY STORY BY ME!

Once upon a time, there was a _____
color

_____ from _____.
animal   faraway place

He rode a _____ to _____
vehicle   store

because he needed to buy _____ cans of
number

_____. "WOW!" said the clerk.
something you buy

"What's an animal like you doing in this store?" The

_____ said, "_____!"
same animal   animal noise

The clerk scratched his head and said, "Why do you

_____

- - - - - - - - - - -

need so many cans of this?" The _____
same animal

answered, "_____!"
another animal sound

The clerk *still* didn't understand. But I did! The

_____

- - - - - - - - -

_____ wanted *all* those cans so it
same animal

_____

- - - - - - - - - - - - -

could _____

_____

- - - - - - - - - - - - - -

_____

THE END.

THE TYPES OF BOOKS AND STORIES I READ

Color in boxes

Paperbacks	Board books
Library books	Graphic novels or comics
Audiobooks	Fact books
Picture books	Books about real people
Early readers	Used books
Encyclopedias	Hardcovers
Fiction	Instruction books
Chapter books	Project books
Digital books	_____

I GET MY BOOKS FROM

Color in answers

A garage sale

My school library

My bookshelf

READ.
A bookshop

The library

Gifts

The school book sale

A thrift shop

Another store

A used bookshop

Online

RAINBOW BOOK COVER HUNT

Can I ☐ find ☐ read a book in each color?

☐ Red   ☐ Green   ☐ Purple
☐ Orange   ☐ Blue   ☐ Black/White
☐ Yellow

Draw each book cover and write the title.

RED

This book is 👍/👎!

ORANGE

This book is 👍 / 👎!

YELLOW

This book is 👍 / 👎!

GREEN

This book is 👍 / 👎 !

BLUE

This book is 👍 / 👎 !

PURPLE

This book is 👍 / 👎!

BLACK/WHITE

This book is 👍 / 👎!

THIS AUTHOR IS **EXCELLENT!**

_____
- -
_____

In two words, their books are

1. _____
- - - - - - - - - - - - - - - - - -
_____

2. _____
- - - - - - - - - - - - - - - - - -
_____

Me reading their books

I ♡ this book they wrote.

Draw covers with titles

Their books make me feel

This book is also 👍.

I GIVE THIS AUTHOR ☆☆☆☆☆ STARS!

iF I OWNED A BOOKSHOP

store name

Fill the
shelves!

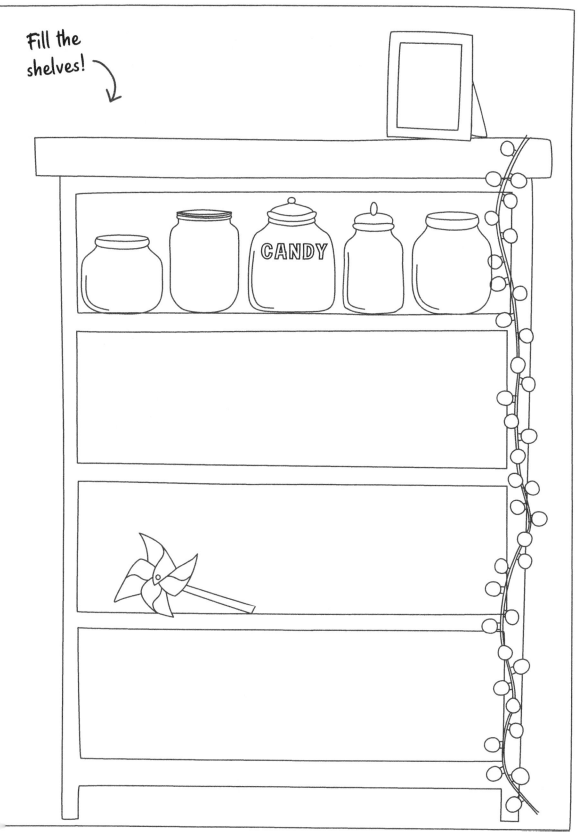

A BOOK RECOMMENDATION FROM

_____

_ _ _ _ _ _ _ _ _ _ _ _ _ _ _

_____

Here they are!

A children's book they really like is

_____

_ _ _ _ _ _ _ _ _ _ _ _ _ _ _

_____

They think it's a great book because

_____

_ _ _ _ _ _ _ _ _ _ _ _ _ _ _

I ☐ have ☐ have not read it.

A BOOK RECOMMENDATION FROM

_____

- - - - - - - - - - - - - - - - -

_____

Here they are!

A children's book they really like is

_____

- - - - - - - - - - - - - - - - -

_____

They think it's a great book because

_____

- - - - - - - - - - - - - - - - -

_____

I ☐ have ☐ have not read it.

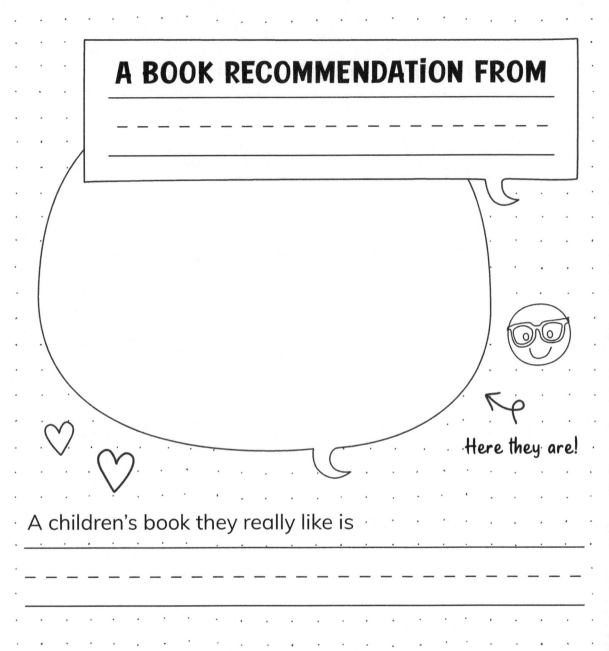

A BOOK RECOMMENDATION FROM

_____

- - - - - - - - - - - - - - - - - -

_____

Here they are!

A children's book they really like is _____

- -

_____

They think it's a fun book because _____

- -

_____

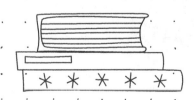

I ☐ have ☐ have not read it.

A BOOK RECOMMENDATION FROM

_____

- - - - - - - - - - - - - - - - - - -

_____

Here they are!

A children's book they really like is

_____

- - - - - - - - - - - - - - - - - - -

_____

They think it's a fun book because

_____

- - - - - - - - - - - - - - - - - - -

_____

I ☐ have ☐ have not read it.

❄ BOOK BINGO ❄

How many ways have I tried reading?
Color or cross off each one. Can I get five in a row?

with a flashlight	in a tree	first thing in the morning	in a laundry basket	while wearing pajamas
during lunch	under a table	in a chair or pillow fort	at some-one else's house	snuggled with a pet
while drinking something warm	in the car	FREE	over the phone or video chat	at the park
in a closet	on the toilet	aloud to someone	on a swing	with a hat on
upside-down	aloud with a funny voice	while on vacation	by a fire	words in another language

IF I WROTE **A BOOK**

My cover
and title

My book would be
☐ Fiction ☐ Nonfiction

The main character's name would be

_____

- - - - - - - - - - - - - - - - - -

_____

The book would be about

_____

- - - - - - - - - - - - - - - - - -

_____

Everyone would say my book is so

_____

- - - - - - - - - - - - - - - - - -

_____

My book would
make kids feel

It'd cost $ _____

- - - - - - - - -

It'd have _____ pages.

People could buy my book at

_____

- - - - - - - - - - - - - - - - - -

_____

DO I KNOW OF...

Draw a picture

A book with a dog in it

A book set in the country

A book with no words

Write the
book title

A book with a train or bus

A book set in the city

A book that makes me think

DO I KNOW OF...

A book that includes a holiday celebration

_____

- -

_____

- -

▭▷ A book that tells a true story

- -

_____

- -

▭▷ A book without any people

- -

_____

- -

I PROBABLY READ

☐ Every day   ☐ Never

☐ Most days   ☐ Only when I'm told to

☐ Some days   ☐ _____

☐ Not very often   _____

I ESTIMATE THE NUMBER OF

☐ Library books in my house

☐ Books on my bed and under my bed

☐ Kid books in my whole house

☐ Books my entire family owns

☐ Books I touch in one day

☐ Minutes I spend with books each day

COLOR AND CUT
PROJECTS

The next pages are paper projects to color, cut, and use

with reading adventures.

Find more (free!)
printables like these at

katieclemons.com/a/2C8Z/

COLOR AND CUT
BOOKMARKS

BUiLD A KEEPSAKE ENVELOPE

 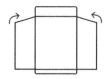

❶ Color and cut out, image facing down.

❷ Fold in side flaps. Glue or tape together.

❸ Fold in bottom flap and adhere.

❹ Fill then fold down top flap.

Tuck into your journal or adhere to the inside cover to hold bookish treasure.

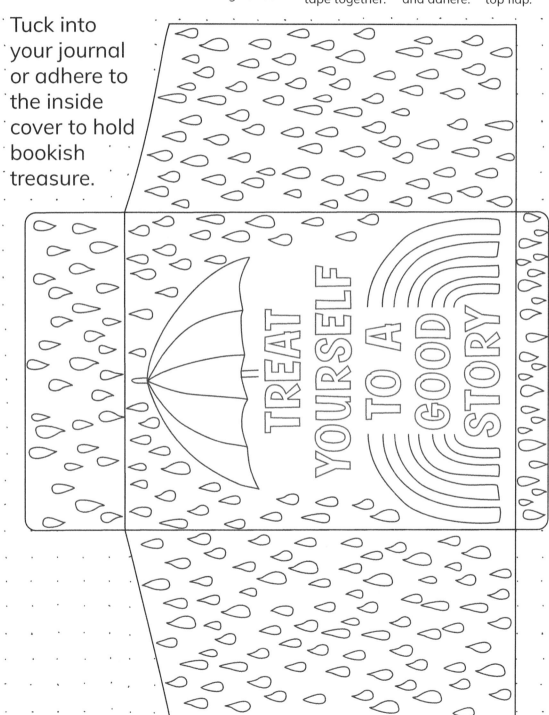

TREAT YOURSELF TO A GOOD STORY

COLOR AND CUT
DOOR HANGER

Adhere your sign to a piece of card-board (such as an old cereal box) to make it stronger.

BOOKiSH NOTES
TO REMEMBER

MY READING LOG

The next 50 pages are for journaling about 25 books I read. Every time I finish a book, I also color in a cloud. How long will it take to fill the pages?

Start date

End date

_____

- - - - - - - - - - - - - - - - - - -

_____

49

BOOK 1

Cover
and
title

In one word,
this book is so _____!

It is ☐ Fiction ☐ Nonfiction

The author's name is

The book is about

The book
makes me feel

I love this
scene or
character.

I GIVE IT ☆☆☆☆☆ STARS!

BOOK 2

Cover
and title

It is ☐ Fiction   ☐ Nonfiction

- ☐ I read this book myself
- ☐ Someone read aloud to me
- ☐ I listened to an audiobook
- ☐ I read back-and-forth with someone
- ☐ _____

The author's name is

_____

_ _ _ _ _ _ _ _ _

_____

The book is about

_____

_ _ _ _ _ _ _ _ _

_____

_____

I love this part of the book.

I GIVE IT ☆☆☆☆☆ STARS!

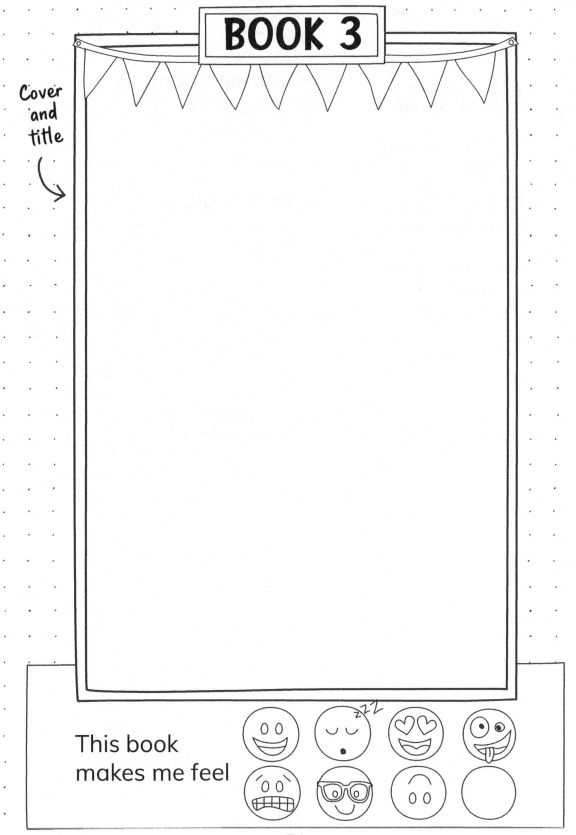

BOOK 3

Cover and title

This book makes me feel

This scene or character is so interesting!

It is ☐ Fiction ☐ Nonfiction

The author's name is

I recommend this book to any kid who

I GIVE IT ☆☆☆☆☆ STARS!

BOOK 4

This book
makes me feel

The author's name is

_____

- - - - - - - - - - - - - - - - -

_____

The book is
☐ Fiction
☐ Nonfiction

The book is about

_____

- - - - - - - - - - - - - - - - -

_____

_____

- - - - - - - - - - - - - - - - -

I love this scene or character.

I GIVE IT ☆☆☆☆☆ STARS!

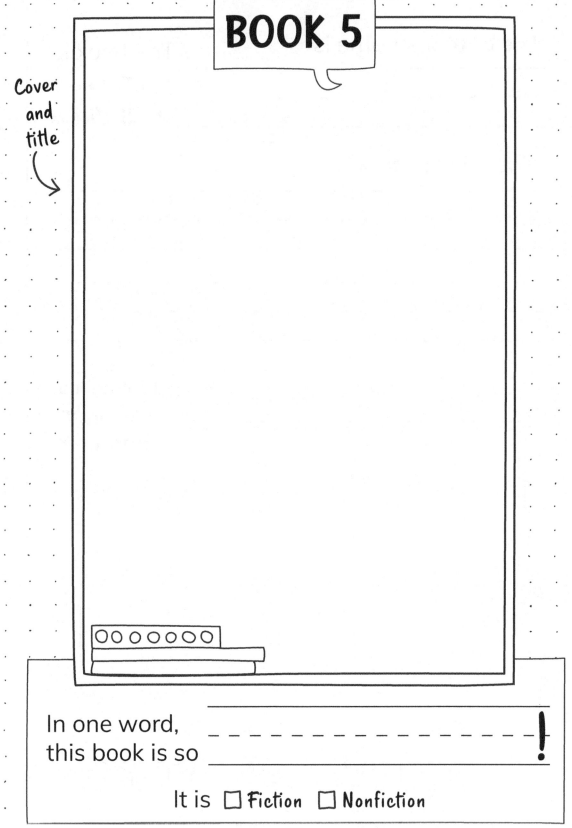

BOOK 5

Cover and title ↘

In one word, this book is so _____!

It is ☐ Fiction ☐ Nonfiction

The author's name is

_____

- - - - - - - - - - - - - - - -

_____

The book is about

_____

- - - - - - - - - - - - - - - -

_____

_____

- - - - - - - - - - - - - - - -

_____

The book
makes me feel

I love this
scene or
character.

I GIVE IT ☆☆☆☆☆ STARS!

BOOK 6

Cover
and title

It is ☐ Fiction ☐ Nonfiction

☐ I read this book myself

☐ Someone read aloud to me

☐ I listened to an audiobook

☐ I read back-and-forth with someone

☐ _____

The author's name is
_____
_ _ _ _ _ _ _ _ _ _ _ _ _
_____

The book is about
_____
_ _ _ _ _ _ _ _ _ _ _ _ _
_____
_ _ _ _ _ _ _ _ _ _ _ _ _
_____

I love this part of the book.

I GIVE IT ☆☆☆☆☆ STARS!

BOOK 7

Cover and title →

This book makes me feel

This scene or character is so interesting!

It is ☐ Fiction ☐ Nonfiction

The author's name is

_____

- - - - - - - - - - - - - - - - - - - -

_____

I recommend this book to any kid who

_____

- - - - - - - - - - - - - - - - - - - -

_____

_____

- - - - - - - - - - - - - - - - - - - -

_____

I GIVE IT ☆☆☆☆☆ STARS!

BOOK 8

This book
makes me feel

The author's name is

_____

- - - - - - - - - - - - - - - - -

_____

The book is
☐ Fiction
☐ Nonfiction

The book is about

_____

- - - - - - - - - - - - - - - - -

_____

_____

- - - - - - - - - - - - - - - - -

_____

* * * * *

I love this scene or character.

I GIVE IT ☆☆☆☆☆ STARS!

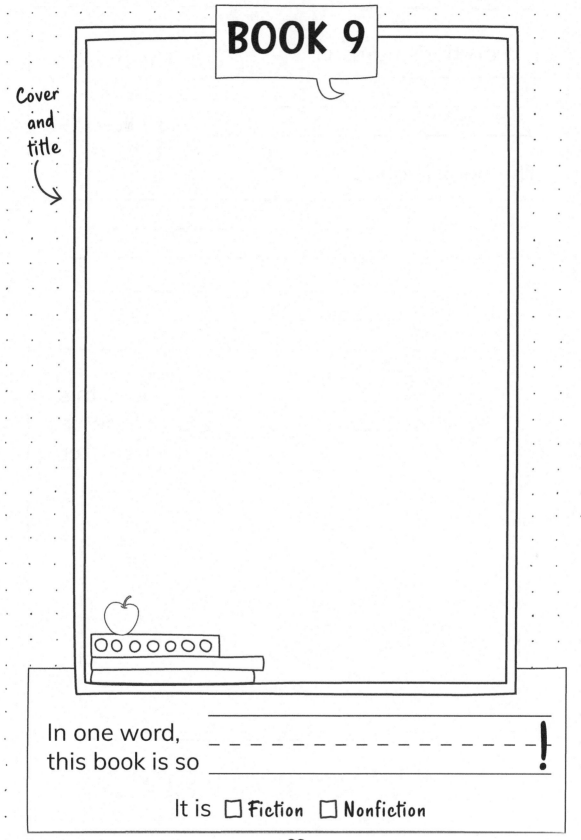

BOOK 9

Cover and title

In one word, this book is so _____!

It is ☐ Fiction ☐ Nonfiction

The author's name is

The book is about

The book makes me feel

I love this scene or character.

I GIVE IT ☆☆☆☆☆ STARS!

BOOK 10

Cover and title

It is ☐ Fiction ☐ Nonfiction

- ☐ I read this book myself
- ☐ Someone read aloud to me
- ☐ I listened to an audiobook
- ☐ I read back-and-forth with someone
- ☐ _____

The author's name is

_____

_____

The book is about

_____

_____

_____

_____

I love this part of the book.

I GIVE IT ☆☆☆☆☆ STARS!

BOOK 11

Cover and title

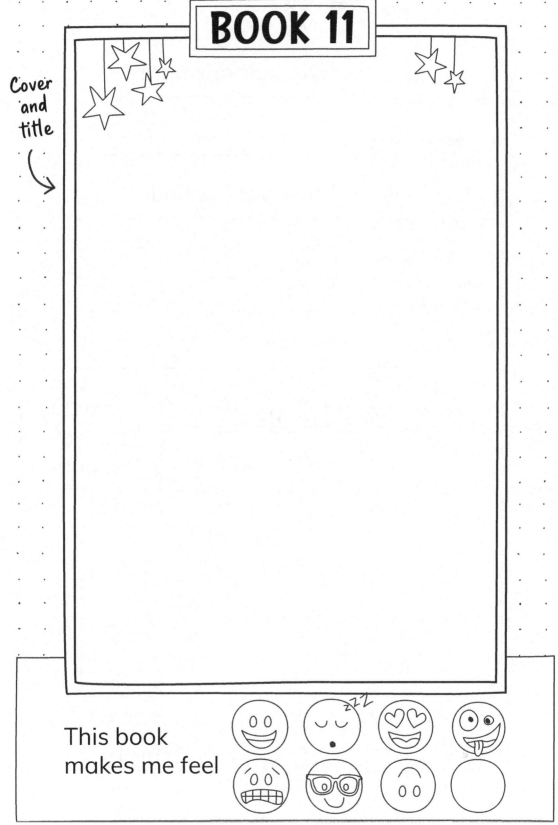

This book makes me feel

This scene or character is so interesting!

It is ☐ Fiction ☐ Nonfiction

The author's name is

_____

- - - - - - - - - - - - - - - - - - - -

_____

I recommend this book to any kid who

_____

- - - - - - - - - - - - - - - - - - - -

_____

_____

- - - - - - - - - - - - - - - - - - - -

_____

I GIVE IT ☆☆☆☆☆ STARS!

BOOK 12

This book makes me feel

The author's name is

_____

- - - - - - - - - - - - - - - - -

_____

The book is
☐ Fiction
☐ Nonfiction

The book is about

_____

- - - - - - - - - - - - - - - - -

_____

- - - - - - - - - - - - - - - - -

_____

I love this scene or character.

I GIVE IT ☆☆☆☆☆ STARS!

BOOK 13

Cover
and
title

In one word,
this book is so _____!

It is ☐ Fiction ☐ Nonfiction

The author's name is

_____

- - - - - - - - - - - -

_____

The book is about

_____

- - - - - - - - - - - -

_____

_____

- - - - - - - - - - - -

_____

The book
makes me feel

I love this
scene or
character.

I GIVE IT ☆☆☆☆☆ STARS!

BOOK 14

Cover and title →

It is ☐ Fiction ☐ Nonfiction

☐ I read this book myself

☐ Someone read aloud to me

☐ I listened to an audiobook

☐ I read back-and-forth with someone

☐ _____

The author's name is
_____
- - - - - - - - - - -
_____

The book is about
_____
- - - - - - - - - - -
_____
_____
_____

I love this part of the book.

I GIVE IT ☆☆☆☆☆ STARS!

BOOK 15

Cover and title ↘

This book makes me feel

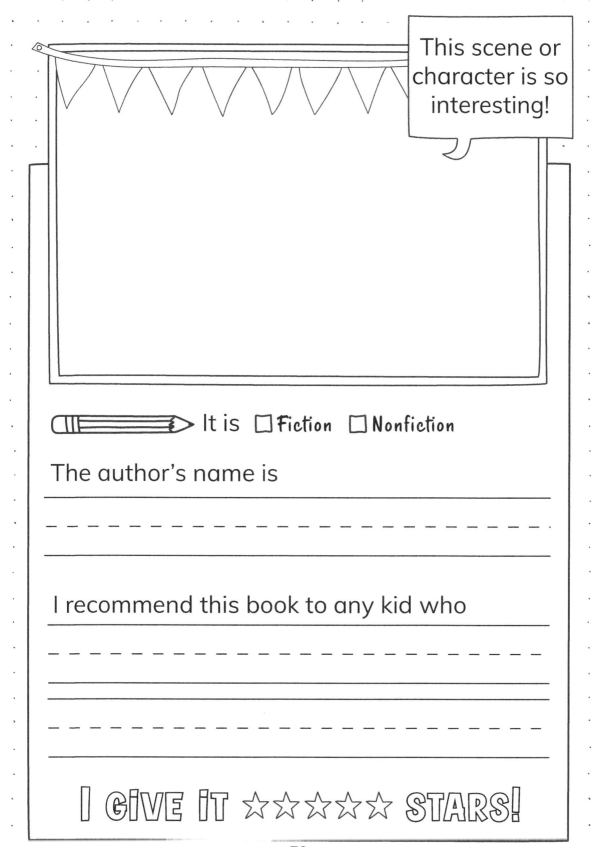

This scene or character is so interesting!

It is ☐ Fiction ☐ Nonfiction

The author's name is

_____

- -

_____

I recommend this book to any kid who

_____

- -

_____
_____

- -

_____

I GIVE IT ☆☆☆☆☆ STARS!

BOOK 16

This book
makes me feel

The author's name is

_____

- - - - - - - - - - - - - -

_____

The book is
☐ Fiction
☐ Nonfiction

The book is about

_____

- - - - - - - - - - - - - -

_____

_____

- - - - - - - - - - - - - -

_____

I love this scene or character.

I GIVE IT ☆☆☆☆☆ STARS!

BOOK 17

Cover
and
title

In one word,
this book is so _____ !

It is ☐ Fiction ☐ Nonfiction

The author's name is

_____

_ _ _ _ _ _ _ _ _ _ _ _ _ _

_____

The book is about

_____

_ _ _ _ _ _ _ _ _ _ _ _ _ _

_____

_____

_ _ _ _ _ _ _ _ _ _ _ _ _ _

The book
makes me feel

I love this
scene or
character.

I GIVE IT ☆☆☆☆☆ STARS!

BOOK 18

Cover
and title

It is ☐ Fiction ☐ Nonfiction

☐ I read this
book myself

☐ Someone read
aloud to me

☐ I listened to
an audiobook

☐ I read back-
and-forth
with someone

☐ _____

The author's name is
_____
- - - - - - - - - - - - - -
_____

The book is about
_____
- - - - - - - - - - - - - -
_____
_____
- - - - - - - - - - - - - -

I love this
part of
the book.

I GIVE IT ☆☆☆☆☆ STARS!

BOOK 19

Cover
and
title

This book
makes me feel

This scene or character is so interesting!

It is ☐ Fiction ☐ Nonfiction

The author's name is

_____

- -

_____

I recommend this book to any kid who

_____

- -

_____

_____

- -

_____

I GIVE IT ☆☆☆☆☆ STARS!

BOOK 20

This book
makes me feel

The author's name is

The book is
☐ Fiction
☐ Nonfiction

The book is about

I love this scene or character.

I GIVE IT ☆☆☆☆☆ STARS!

BOOK 21

Cover and title →

In one word, this book is so _____!

It is ☐ Fiction ☐ Nonfiction

The author's name is

_____

– – – – – – – – – – – – – – –

_____

The book is about

_____

– – – – – – – – – – – – – – –

_____

_____

– – – – – – – – – – – – – – –

_____

The book
makes me feel

I love this
scene or
character.

I GIVE IT ☆☆☆☆☆ STARS!

BOOK 22

Cover and title

It is ☐ Fiction ☐ Nonfiction

- ☐ I read this book myself
- ☐ Someone read aloud to me
- ☐ I listened to an audiobook
- ☐ I read back-and-forth with someone
- ☐ _____

The author's name is
_____
- - - - - - - - - - -
_____

The book is about
_____
- - - - - - - - - - -
_____
- - - - - - - - - - -

I love this part of the book.

* * * * *

I GIVE IT ☆☆☆☆☆ STARS!

BOOK 23

Cover
and
title

This book
makes me feel

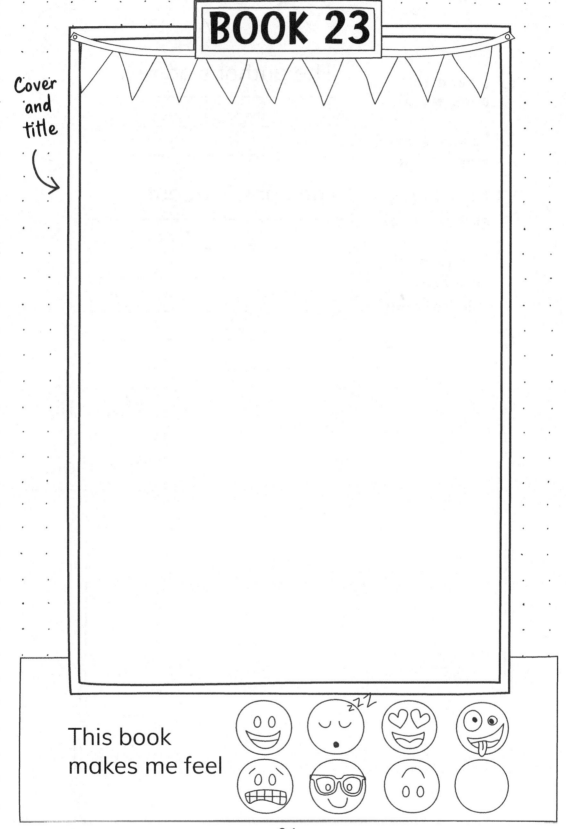

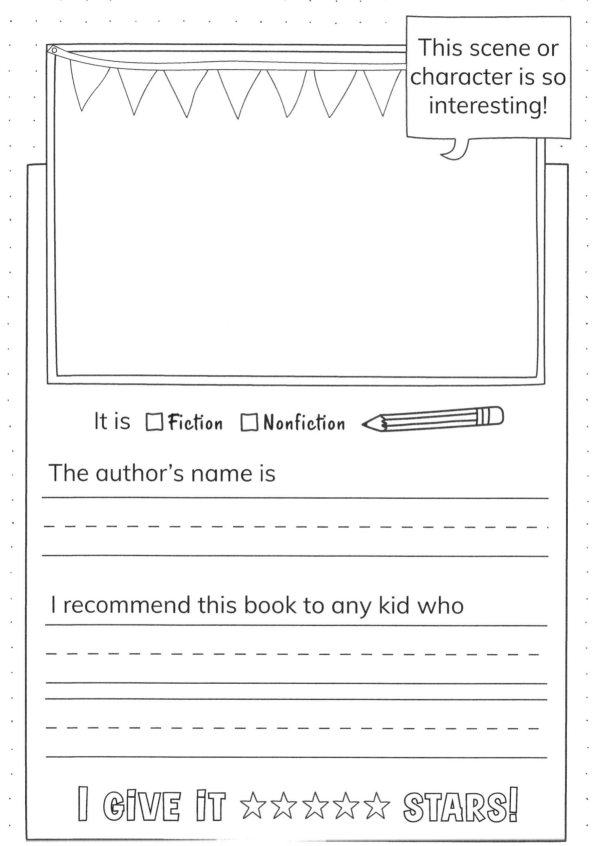

This scene or character is so interesting!

It is ☐ Fiction ☐ Nonfiction

The author's name is

_____

- -

_____

I recommend this book to any kid who

_____

- -

_____

_____

- -

_____

I GIVE IT ☆☆☆☆☆ STARS!

BOOK 24

This book
makes me feel

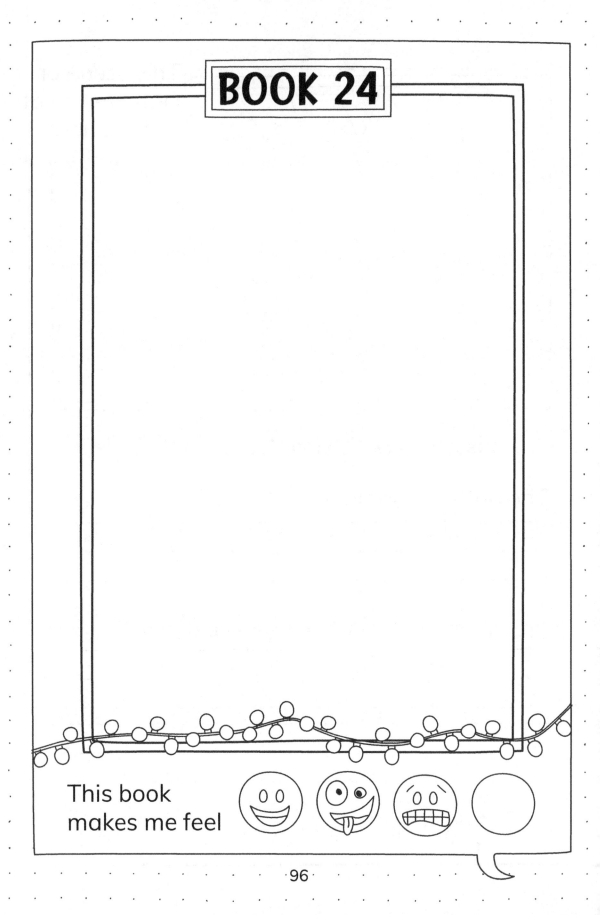

The author's name is

_____

- - - - - - - - - - - - - - -

_____

The book is
☐ Fiction
☐ Nonfiction

The book is about

_____

- - - - - - - - - - - - - - -

_____

- - - - - - - - - - - - - - -

_____

I love this scene or character.

I GIVE IT ☆☆☆☆☆ STARS!

BOOK 25

Cover
and
title

In one word,
this book is so _____ !

It is ☐ Fiction ☐ Nonfiction

The author's name is

_____

– – – – – – – – – – – –

_____

The book is about

– – – – – – – – – – – –

_____

– – – – – – – – – – – –

_____

– – – – – – – – – – – –

_____

The book
makes me feel

I love this
scene or
character.

I GIVE IT ☆☆☆☆☆ STARS!

THE END . . . ALMOST.

☐ I've read 25 books.

☐ I've written to the end of this journal.

Here's one last
picture of me

While keeping this journal, I learned

_____

_ _

_____

My favorite memory recorded in this journal is

_____

_ _

_____

☐ **OKAY, NOW I'M FINISHED!**

LET'S CELEBRATE MORE OF YOUR STORY!

I I believe your story is one of the most meaningful gifts you can give yourself. THANK YOU for entrusting me and this journal during your reading adventures.

Let's keep collecting your stories—I call it storycatching, and we'll do it together. Join me at **katieclemons.com** to see my entire collection of books and projects. Below are a few treasures you might especially enjoy!

KEEPSAKE JOURNALS FOR KiDS

TiME CAPSULE
A Seriously Awesome
Kid's Journal

BETWEEN MOM AND ME
A Mother & Son Keepsake
Journal*

LOVE, MOM AND ME
A Mother & Daughter
Keepsake Journal*

HERE I GO!
A Travel Journal

WE ARE SO THANKFUL
An Adult & Child
Gratitude Journal

OUR PRAYER JOURNAL
An Adult & Child Christian
Prayer Journal

LOGBOOKS FOR KiDS

KiD'S CAMPING JOURNAL

*Editions
for **KiDS** to share with
DAD, **GRANDMA**, and
GRANDPA too!

Kid journals

Bookish freebies

Made in United States
Orlando, FL
02 July 2025

62576705R00057